Jack-A-Bee 20 Milestone Challenges: Outdoor & Activity

Jack-A-Bee Milestones for Outdoor Fun, Socialisation, Agility, Training

Volume 1

Todays Doggy

Copyright © 2023

All rights reserved. Without limiting rights under the copyright reserved above, no part of this publication may be reproduced, stored, introduced into a retrieval system, distributed or transmitted in any form or by any means, including without limitation photocopying, recording, or other electronic or mechanical methods, without the prior written permission of the publisher, except in the case of brief quotations embodied in critical reviews and certain other non-commercial uses permitted by copyright law.

The scanning, uploading, and/or distribution of this document via the internet or via any other means without the permission of the publisher is illegal and is punishable by law. Please purchase only authorized editions and do not participate in or encourage electronic piracy of copyrightable materials

Dedicated To All of You Wonderful Owners and Fans

Introduction

Welcome to the Original Doggy Milestone Series™ where you are encouraged to create those special moments with your pup. We have composed the milestones in a way that challenges you to set the stage before taking your photos.

Use props and make it fun - be creative in setting up your photos. Get family and friends involved - take it out with you - use it in different places and settings - have a play with it and most importantly, have a good time!

Good luck and enjoy your photo fun.

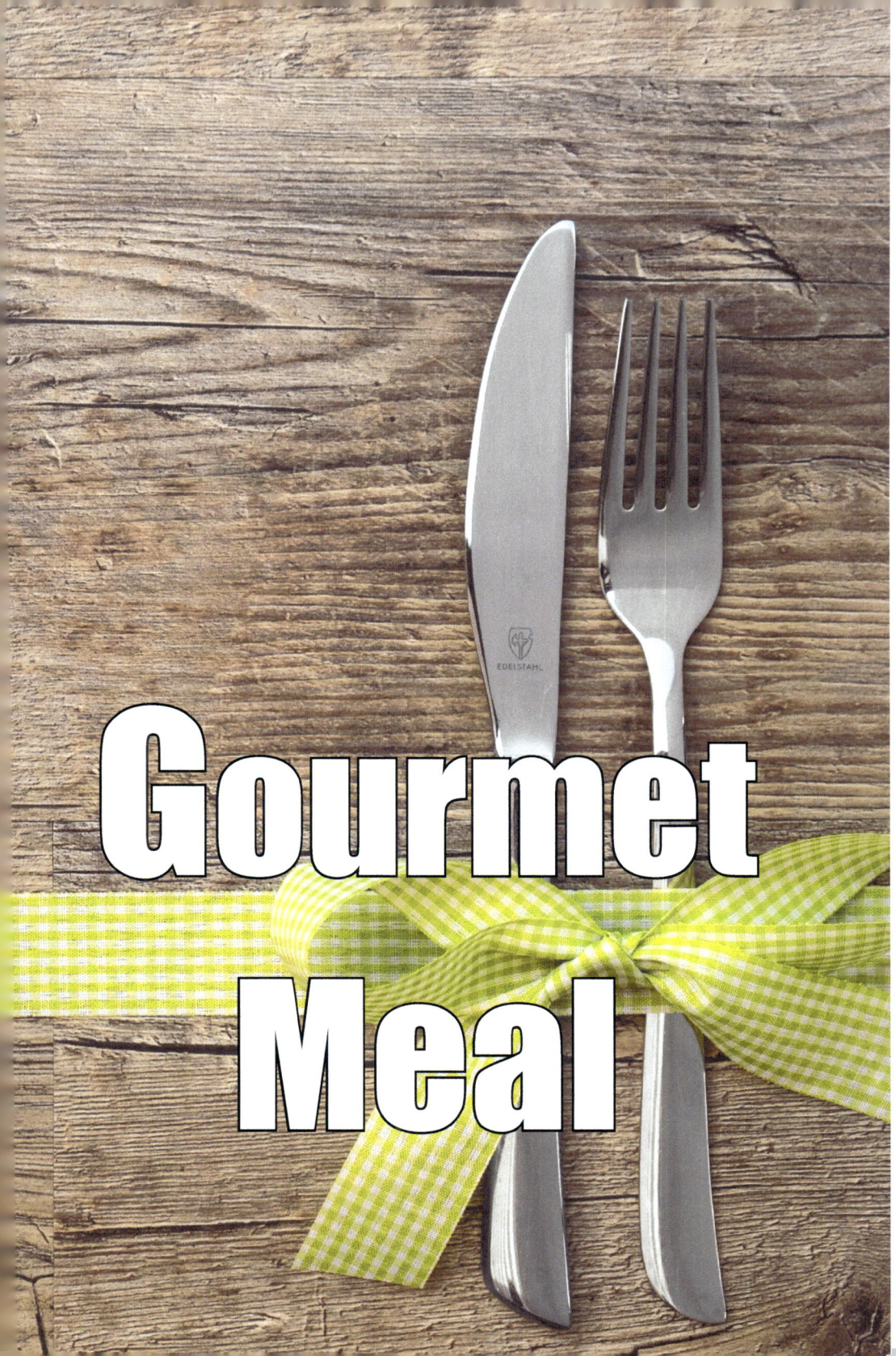

Cats LOVE Me

Look at my

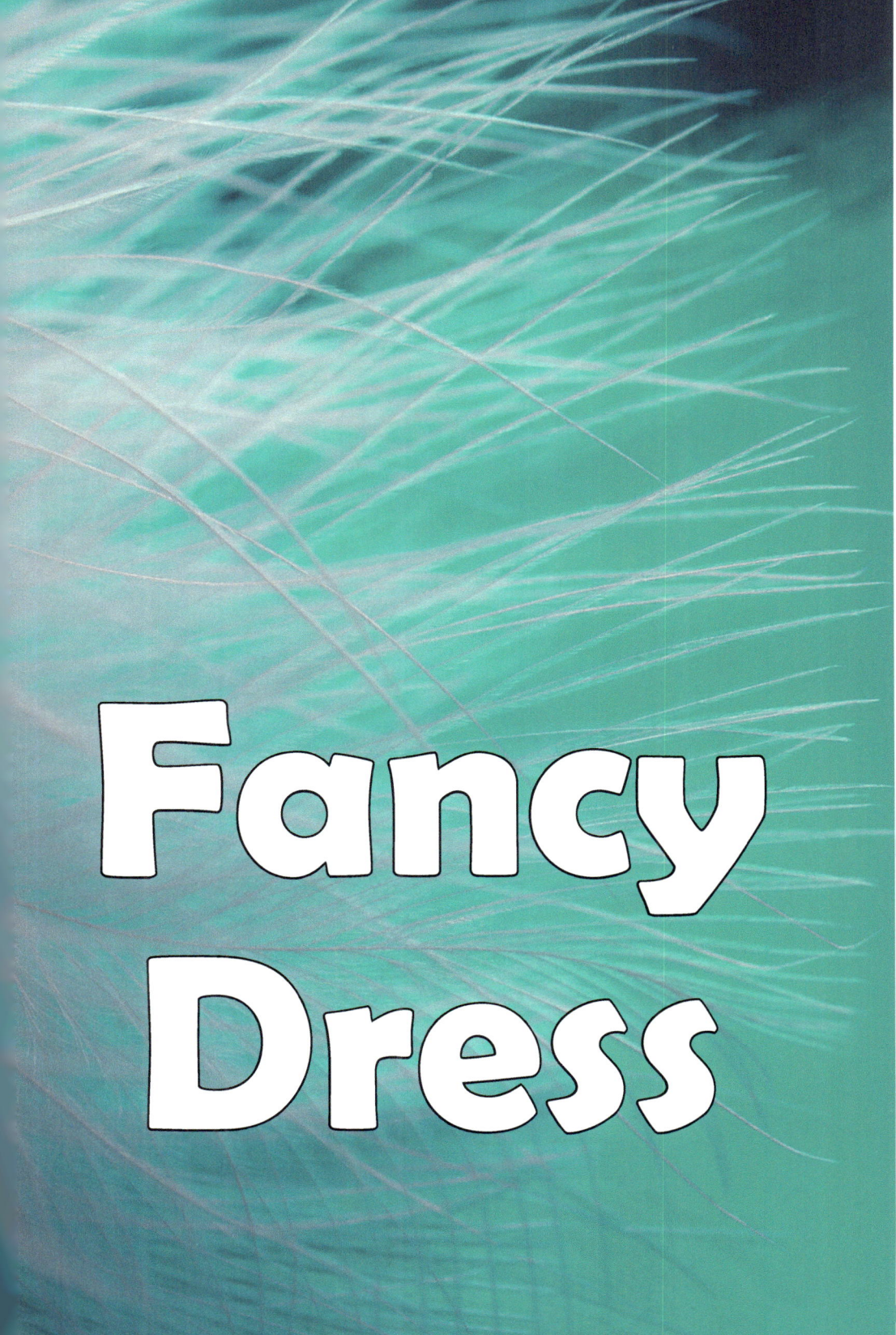

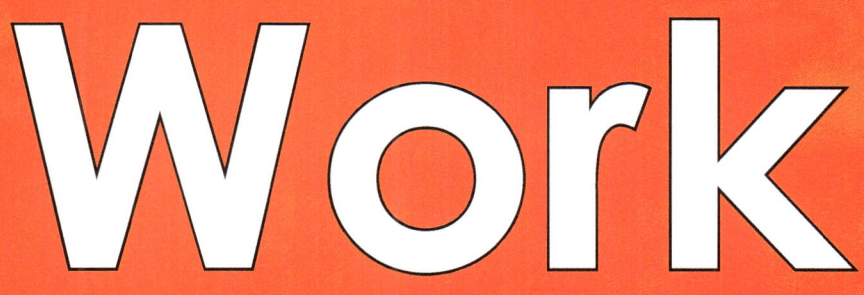

This Paddle Board is

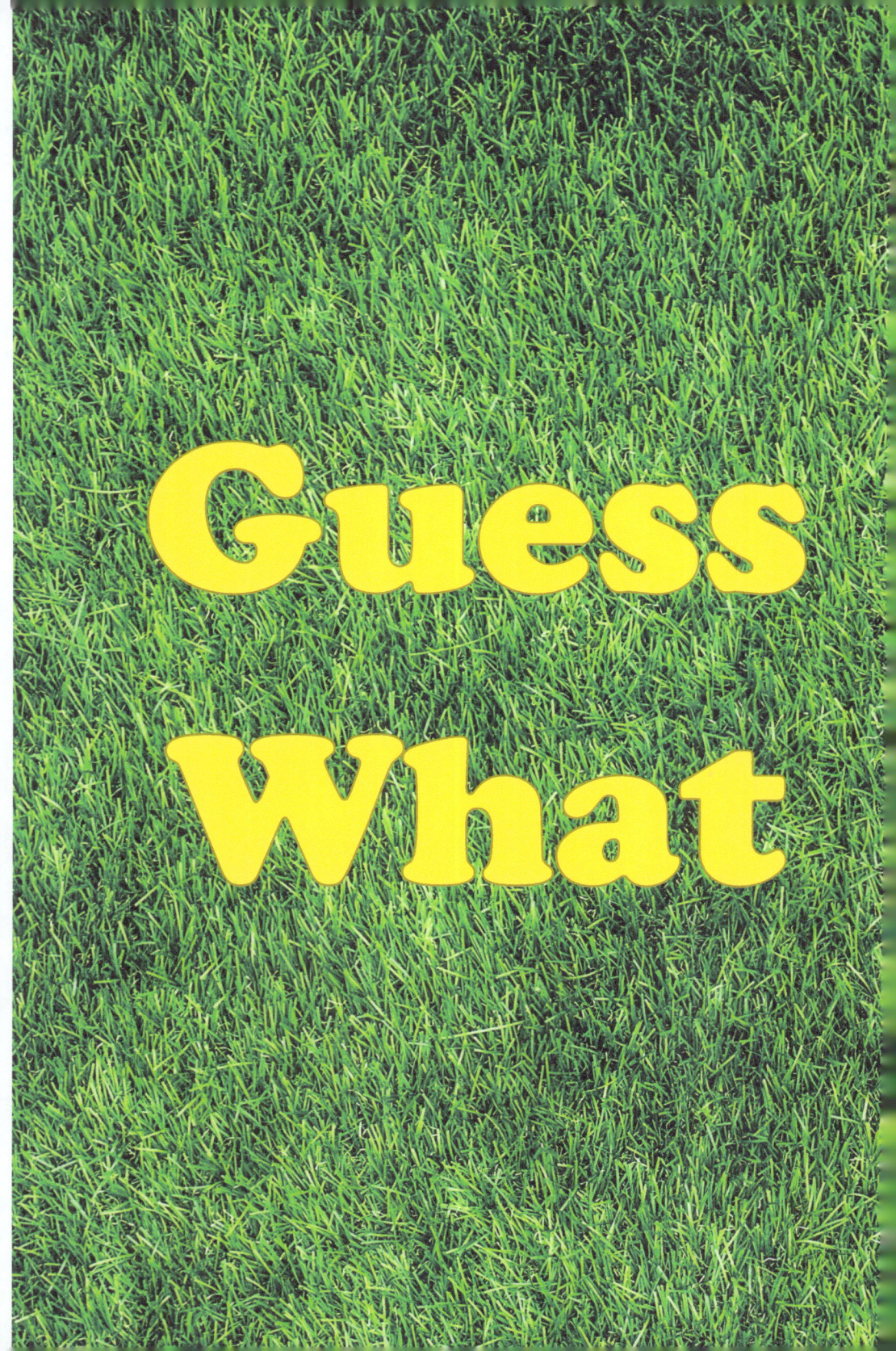

My Favourite Sport Is?

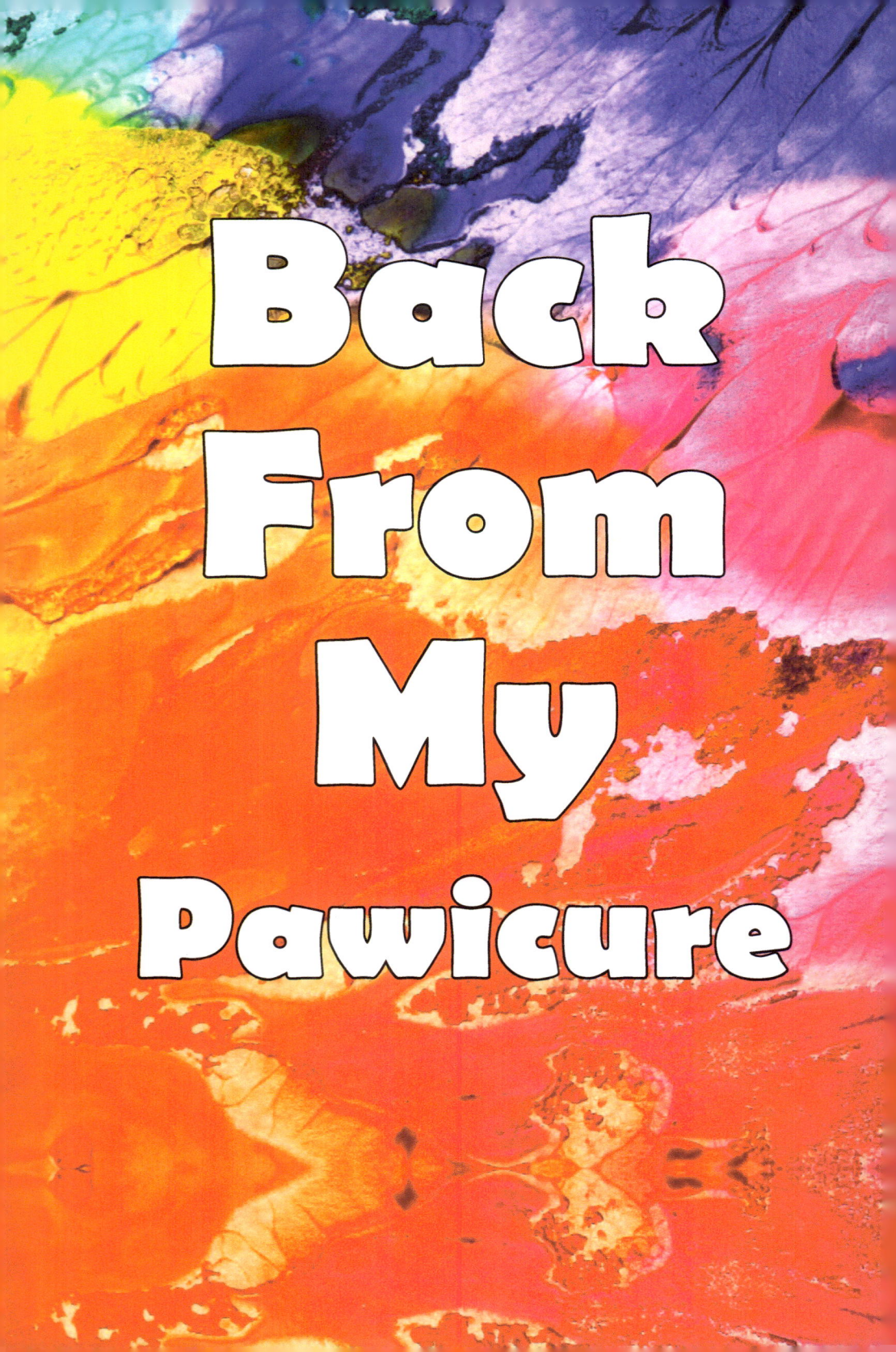

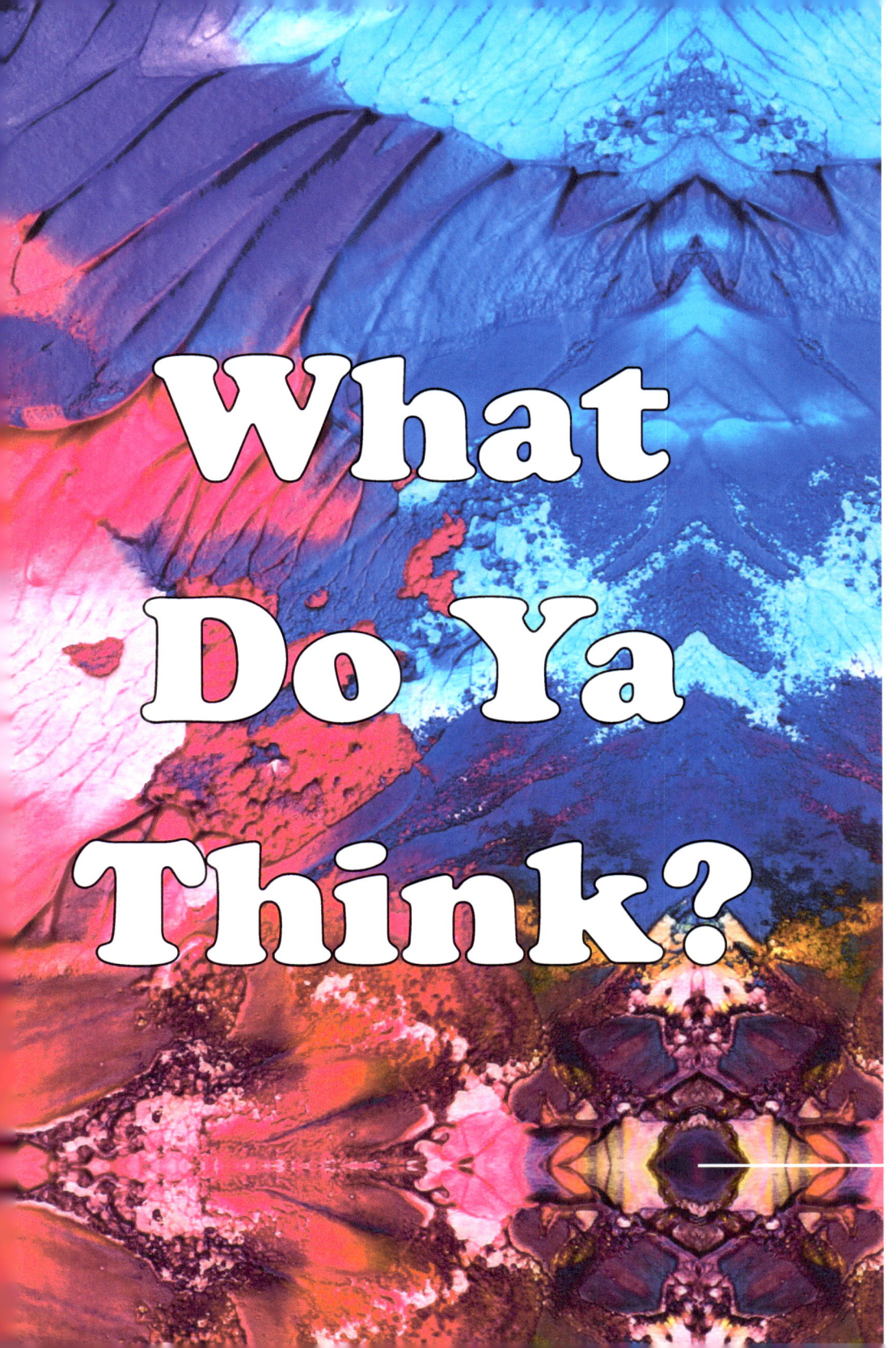

You Found Me!

LOST

FOUND

SEARCHING

Hide & Seek is Fun

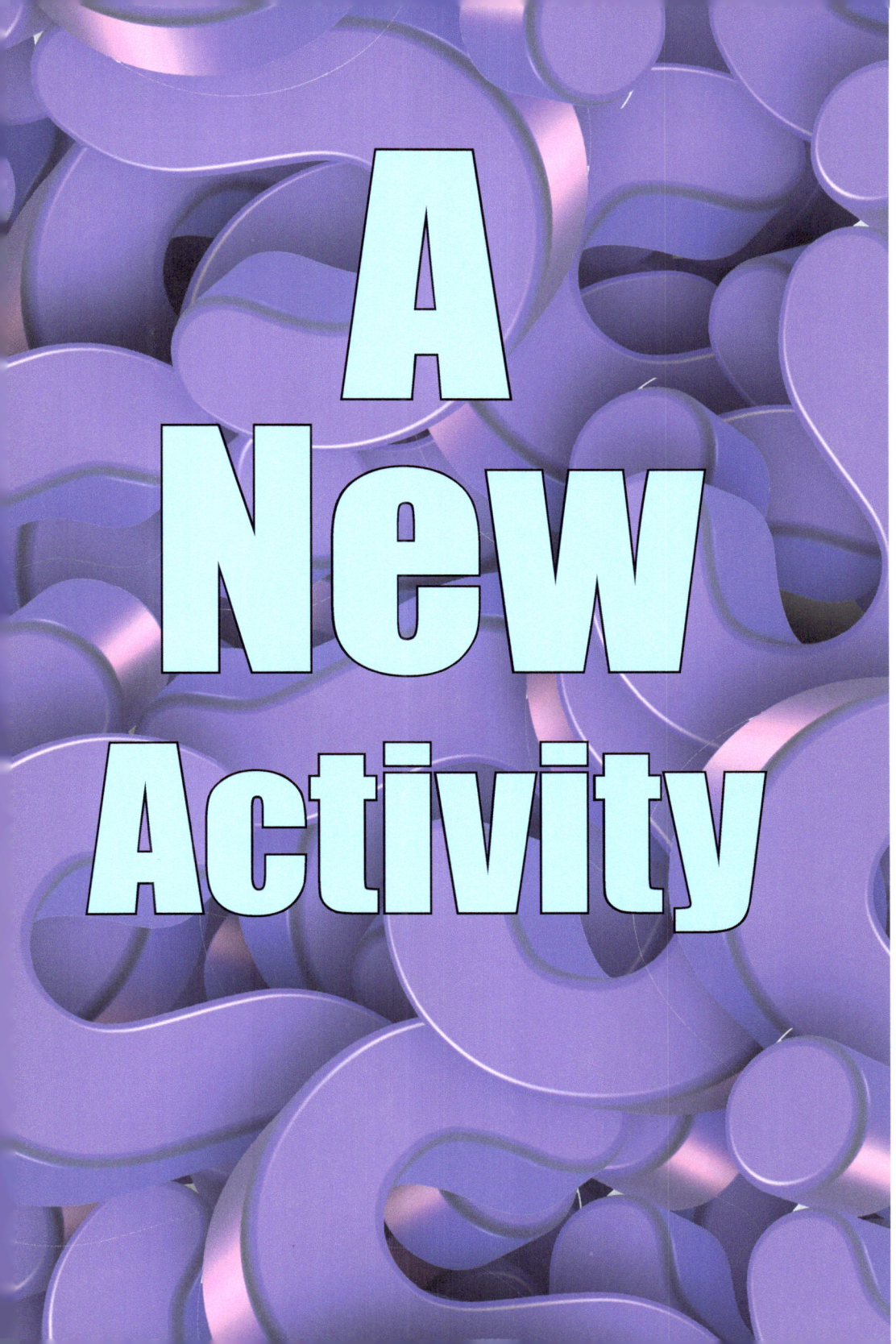

Agility Training Today

Visiting a

Food Glorious Food!

The Hammock

Where Dreams Are Made

Went Exploring

Look What I Found

DOGGY YOGA

My Best Pose

www.ingramcontent.com/pod-product-compliance
Lightning Source LLC
Chambersburg PA
CBHW041510010526
44118CB00006B/214